Key Notes

Creative Steps to Piano Success

by Barbara Wing

American Literary Press
Five Star Special Edition
Baltimore, Maryland

Key Notes:
Creative Steps to Piano Success

Copyright © 2006 Barbara Wing

Library of Congress
Cataloging-in-Publication Data
ISBN 1-56167-935-6

Library of Congress Card Catalog Number:
2006902828

American Literary Press
Five Star Special Edition
8019 Belair Road, Suite 10
Baltimore, Maryland 21236

Manufactured in the United States of America

CONTENTS

Prelude

Occasionally I have had a parent say to me during a student interview, "I would like my child to learn to play the piano, but I do not want him to become a concert pianist". And then I think, reflecting on the child's average musicality, "Don't worry, it could never happen."

But my next thought is that a young student could aspire to be a piano teacher as it is a very satisfying career. Alternatively, he could continue his music study as an adult amateur musician. It is true that to be a teacher, he would need to study seriously, and play artistically, but other facets of teaching, such as helping a young musician become the best he can be, are equally as important and supremely rewarding.

This book is written for those who teach music to others, as a career, and also for those amateur musicians who learn music by themselves. Since teaching and learning are two sides of the same coin, there are creative steps for each of these musicians in every chapter.

When I look back over my career as a musician and teacher, I know I have learned as much from my students as from my teachers. They have taught me that building on one's successes can be even more powerful than fixing weaknesses. The reason has much to do with self-image and confidence, both healthy indicators of future success in any field.

I remember teaching a music class, years ago, with three students. who each had their own reason for self-confidence. Meghan was the best performer, Liz had the sharpest ear and Justin had the broadest knowledge of music. Which was the best student? Each would have chosen himself. All three students felt they excelled in music, which they did, but each in their own way.

In my 40+ years of teaching, several threads have woven together to form a strong teaching philosophy. Many are reflected in the chapters of this book.

First and foremost is that there is music in everyone and it is our challenge and opportunity as teachers to bring it to life however it presents itself. As each student's gift is unique to himself, one cannot have a "one size fits all" teaching curriculum. One must search for repertoire and teaching methods that fit each child and encourage self expression within the bounds of stylistic integrity.

Secondly, whereas competitiveness is a stimulant to some students, and certainly a mainstay of our society's lifestyle, it is not always right or even necessary for many. One might say that music provides a balance, a relief from the competitive world of sports and academics, and has value precisely for that reason. Certainly the many adults who return to music study in later years would attest to this.

Thirdly, I believe in music lessons and not solely piano lessons. Students should have a thorough grounding in music theory which goes beyond the reciting of fundamentals and reaches into exploring how and why a composer crafted his composition the way he did. What makes it expressive? Was it innovative at the time it was written? What other types of music did the composer write and did this influence his piano music or was it the other way around? Students should develop a curiosity about the life and times of these musicians much as they study history and literature in school. These discussions can happen easily in a piano class or whenever a student learns a new piece.

Whereas much of our teaching repertoire centers around historic musical styles, a teacher should help students relate to their own generation as well. Many students want to study pieces that will impress their peers at school talent shows. Others want some familiarity with jazz so that they can audition for the middle school jazz band. Sightreading skills help students who wish to accompany their school choruses or the high school musical. Some students wish to compose their own music, much as their guitar playing friends are doing. Realize that when a student seeks to promote his musical identity in school, it is an indication that he values his musical life highly. It is worth helping him succeed.

Most importantly, I feel that a career in teaching piano is more about teaching the student than it is about teaching music, or teaching the piano. Just as in a performance, it is a chance to share a love of music with another human being. Every lesson is different because every student brings something unique to the studio. Build on this uniqueness and create a curriculum that both satisfies and stretches each individual, whether adult or child.

Publicly, music study rewards the best performers. Explicitly through competitions, and less explicitly through recitals, we tend to admire the students who play the most difficult repertoire. Contrary to this, few adults either can or want to perform their youthful recital pieces once they are grown up, but choose more appropriate repertoire. Sidney Lawrence, director of the Harbor Conservatory for Musical Growth, Long Island, NY, discovered, through questioning the parents of his school students, that primarily those who had previously learned to sightread or improvise were still playing the piano as adults. These people had become independent of their teachers, and no longer needed someone to guide their every step. They were able to continue playing on their own. Others stopped playing long ago.

Since few of us are likely to train future concert pianists, is it unrealistic to hope that every one of our students will continue to play the piano as amateur adults? This must be our primary objective. We must relate our teaching to the needs and interests of individual students. By teaching sightreading and ensemble skills, we are preparing them for many delightful evenings of chamber music. By discussing the lives of composers and the structure of the music, we are preparing them to understand the concerts they attend and the music they play at home. By teaching them to improvise, we may be helping them relax after a busy and stressful workday. By being an exemplary teacher, they may follow in our footsteps.

This is not to negate performance skills. These will

always be at the core of what we teach. I remember attending a high school "career night" where several professional musicians addressed the young attendees and their parents. On the panel were a teacher, a concert performer, a music journalist, a proprietor of a music store and an announcer on a music radio station. As each recounted his life story, each panelist emphasized the importance of having mastered a performing instrument as an essential prerequisite to his current musical career. This gave each of them the credibility to interact effectively with professional musicians. which they did frequently.

Many of our students will not choose a musical career but will continue their piano playing as an avocation. We need to teach them skills so they can do this.

Hopefully some may aspire to be a piano teacher, which is a very fulfilling career. First of all, it is creative, requiring appropriate lesson plans for each individual student. Secondly, it encourages continuous personal growth. Through studying new repertoire, one discovers additional insights into the music and effective ways to master it.

Finally, helping someone grow intellectually, emotionally and in physical skills, is wholly satisfying. Working with people and music every day is what makes this particular career so fulfilling. I highly recommend it.

The names in this book are entirely fictitious. They are intended to bear no resemblance to any student past or present. The pronouns he or she are intended to apply to either gender. This may be obvious, but needs to be stated.

Barbara Wing

I wish to acknowledge the many friends, colleagues and family members who read portions of this book, and the many students over the years, who gave inspiration for writing it.

A Sound Beginning
A New Approach to Teaching Beginners in Piano Study

Do you ever wonder why, with all the emphasis given to teaching reading by our current method books, we still do not develop good fluent readers among our students? And it is worth wondering how students can develop a sense of the expressive quality of music, while practicing, week after week, pieces restricted to the few notes their method books have taught them.

I believe there is a better way to begin music study, one that balances expressive playing with secure reading. This approach ensures that a student really understands the components of both reading and playing music, and leads him toward learning music independently.

There are two meanings to "A Sound Beginning", the title of this chapter. The first is a reminder that what music sounds like, its expressive nature, must be conveyed to students at the beginning of their lessons. The second underscores the belief that this approach creates the strongest foundation for success in further music study.

This chapter describes the approach by presenting three skills to be taught independently of each other. These are:
- Learning to play expressive pieces by ear
- Reading rhythmic phrases fluently on a single piano key
- Reading melodies by direction and interval rather than by note names

We cannot assume that all beginning students will continue study for a long time. Competing interests, lack of sufficient practice time, or family finances may limit the years that a student may study piano. Understand this, and be sure that each student acquires the necessary reading, theoretical and technical skills to continue playing independently at his current level.

Traditionally, beginning students must master many elements of playing at the same time: correct notes, rhythm, fingering, hand position, dynamics etc. If instead they master these separately, before combining them, students progress much faster and play with much more security and musicality.

To begin with, students learn expressive pieces by ear. These are short pieces, meant to describe, through sound, the meaning of the title. They differ from each other in dynamics, tempo and style. Students are taught what to do technically to make these differences heard.

How to choose pieces to teach by ear.

Central to my instruction are the "Sound Pictures", a set of original pieces which promote expressive play-

ing. Teachers can also choose imaginative pieces by any author. A good "Sound Picture" must be:
- short enough to teach quickly, and be retained by the student without any notation;
- designed to tell a story or describe a visual image;
- "patterned" or made up of easy to remember musical elements.

Teaching by ear – how to do it.
- Play the new piece for the student
- Describe and analyze through guided questions
- Student copies, section by section
- Suggest how to enhance sound of the piece

At the beginning of a lesson, play the new piece. One section at a time, ask the student to describe what he hears, and then try it himself. Continue, one section at a time, until he can play the whole piece. Describing the piece helps him remember what to play, as he cannot yet read music. Learning by ear satisfies his desire to play a piece immediately, while helping develop his listening and memory, two essential skills in piano study.

Teach your beginning student a new piece by ear at every lesson. When he has learned many of these pieces, he will have played a wide dynamic range on all parts of the keyboard. This is immensely more satisfying than being limited to one or two hand positions as in many primers.

A Sample "Sound Picture."

I Like Popcorn

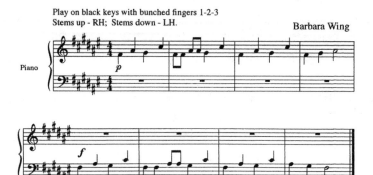

Play on black keys with bunched fingers 1-2-3
Stems up - RH; Stems down - LH.

Barbara Wing

I like popcorn; Yummy, yummy popcorn,

I like popcorn; Yes, I do!

Here's some popcorn; Yummy, yummy popcorn,

Here's some popcorn, Just for you.

How to Teach "I Like Popcorn."

"I Like Popcorn", can be introduced through an improvised story of a visit to a movie theater where a student delights in purchasing a large container of popcorn before watching the movie. Demonstrate the piece on black keys, with a firm staccato touch, imitating the "pop" of a popcorn machine.

Ask the student what he sees or hears in the performance. Guided by his response, help him discover, by further questioning, how the piece is constructed and invite him to try it out. Playing all the black keys with a cluster of fingers 1,2 and 3 forms a perfect hand position and allows the student to use his larger arm muscles, since individual finger coordination is as yet undeveloped.

At subsequent lessons, teach a new "Sound Picture", each differing from previous pieces in mood, style and technique.

Over several months students easily build a repertoire of many "Sound Pictures". They play these at each lesson allowing the teacher to continually improve how they sound.

Later in the lesson, assign rhythm reading and eventually melody reading exercises, developing skills in each of these areas independently. After several months, these three areas, playing expressively, rhythm reading and melody reading converge, and the student can now read and play successfully and independently music from any first year book.

Use this approach with beginners of all ages. Its logic appeals to adult beginners and you can easily adapt the pacing to suit young students as well.

Teaching rhythm reading exercises – how to do it.

- Show the student how to play with a braced third finger
- Assign a single piano key for each hand
- Set the tempo by playing several beats in a low register
- Check that eyes are on the page
- Accompany your student so he never stops.

A Sample "Tapping Page"

Tapping page

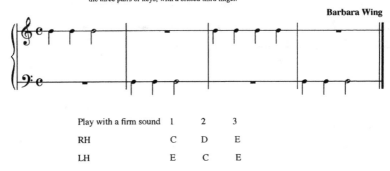

This is a sample first lesson for a beginning student learning
CDE on the keyboard. Each 4-bar phrase is practiced 3 times, using
the three pairs of keys, with a braced third finger.

Barbara Wing

Play with a firm sound	1	2	3
RH		C	D	E
LH		E	C	E

Use the Tapping Pages for:
- Young Beginners
  - Adult Beginners
    - Remedial Reading Exercises

After the Sound Picture, teach your student to read music through rhythm and reading exercises, which can be found in my books "Rhythm and Reading". or composed by a teacher. Reading exercise lessons begin with rhythm phrases and, after several weeks, proceed to short melodies.

The four-bar rhythm exercises each feature a relationship between two note values. In the first exercise those note values are the quarter note and the half note. The student selects two piano keys, one key for each hand, and plays the exercise with a braced third finger. He puts his thumb behind the first joint of the third finger, which curls around the thumb and points into the key. Notice he is playing with a proper hand position. Keeping eyes firmly on the page, he reads and plays fluently from left to right. There is no need to look at the keyboard since his hands do not move out of position.

Teaching rhythm reading through a four bar phrase builds fluency. Students count aloud as they play, and can be accompanied by their teacher in a lower octave.

The progression of rhythm exercises presents all combinations of two note and rest values. Decide how quickly or slowly to advance through the exercises. You may even choose to suspend the rhythm exercises for a while, and resume them a little later when your student is ready for compound meter or sixteenth notes.

How to teach pitch reading by direction and interval.

- Relate up, down, same to sound and direction on keys as well as to note placement on the staff
- Teach 2nds, 5ths, 3rds then 4ths
- Accompany student so he keeps playing fluently

Reading Exercise

After several lessons using only rhythm exercises, begin the melody reading exercises. These are also four bar phrases that feature reading by direction and interval. Again, students keep their eyes on the page. Each phrase has an identical rhythm pattern so that all attention is on pitch movement. The exercises first present only the interval of a second with all notes in the phrase being either a second higher or lower than the previous notes. Subsequent exercises introduce fifths, thirds and fourths.

Students learn to read intervals on both staffs before they learn the names of the lines and spaces.

This is a unique approach. Good musicians read music by patterns, which are combinations of intervals, much as one reads by words or phrases rather than by individual letters. Students must learn to read by patterns, rather than by looking at each note and thinking of its name. Therefore, delay teaching the names of notes on the staff until students are very secure reading intervals. When they do learn the note names, reinforce these lessons with games, playing in group classes or with their parents at home.

Easy as One, Two, Three - a Note Reading Game

Prepare three sets of flash cards. Each card in Set One will have three notes in the vicinity of Treble C; Set Two with notes surrounding Middle C; and Set Three with notes around Bass C. Write the number one, two or three on the back of the cards, corresponding to these sets, which indicate points to be earned.

Place the three sets face down on a table. Ask your student to select a card. If he reads it correctly, he earns the points on the back of the card. Continue with other students, or with the teacher and parent.

This game can be played in a group, where the

winner is the student with the most points. If played with a teacher or parent, then the student wins when he reaches 50 points or an agreed upon goal.

What comes next? Hands together.

The process of teaching A Sound Beginning, ("Sound Pictures" and "Rhythm and Reading" exercises) takes about one semester. By this time, students can read single handed pieces from any primer book.

Learning to read and play hands together literature is not too different from the above, but requires extra practice due to the coordination problem of playing two hands at the same time. It is better to establish secure reading habits with alternating hands before moving to hands together literature. The reward comes soon enough when your student is totally confident in reading music and is ready to undertake technical challenges, such as hands together playing.

Use with transfer students who are weak in reading.

The approach works well remedially as a "Speed reading course" with transfer students who play better than they read.. Proceed more slowly for a young student or more quickly for an older student. Choose age appropriate "Sound Pictures" to appeal to each individual.

It is also a model for how to learn new repertoire. When assigning new music, use what is now a familiar approach. Tap the rhythm first, while looking for patterns, to be sure there will be no rhythmic errors in practicing. Then scan for intervals before beginning to play. This process helps a student avoid mistakes in the early stages of learning, which can come back to haunt him in a performance later on. Once the brain has learned something wrong, it is not easy to permanently eradicate the error.

Too many students terminate lessons within the first few years of study. They may feel frustration over learning new music, or be bored with the uninteresting music they are assigned to play. Mastering one area of reading at a time while learning to play expressively by ear ought to keep those students in music study a lot longer. They will have the skills and devotion to enjoy music for the rest of their lives.

Practicing for Progress & Pleasure

"I love to play the piano but I hate to practice", say some younger students. "I love to practice but I hate to perform", reply some adult students. This leads one to believe that maturity level has a lot to do with one's enjoyment of practicing, and perhaps effectiveness of learning as well.

In other fields, hours are happily spent refining skills. A young basketball player enjoys the time he spends throwing balls at the basketball hoop. A chef delights in experimenting at the kitchen stove. A model builder derives much pleasure from seeing his ship emerge from the many tiny parts that go into its construction.

No one is born knowing how to practice the piano, so it is the teacher's role to instruct students in efficient and effective ways to develop their skills and master their literature. Here is an overview of what is required, and suggestions to make this process as pleasurable as possible.

Fall in love with your music

First, one needs to fall in love with the music. Taking a holistic approach, one must feel an emotional response to what the music is saying, creating a desire to reproduce it. This can be done by attending a concert during which a professional artist gives a magnificent performance. Listening to a CD can give almost the same feeling, though visually watching a performance gives an added dimension that is very invigorating.

Young students can fall in love with their new pieces by listening to their teacher perform it for them. Therefore it is necessary that the teacher be a very good pianist. If she plays haltingly, or makes many errors, it is unlikely to impress the student with the beauty of the music. Alternatively, a student musician can sight-read the new piece, with the intent of discovering its emotional tone, rather than being concerned with technical accuracy. Since eventually amateur pianists become their own teachers, it is wise to develop sight-reading skills so they can do this.

When listening to, or reading a new piece, become aware of its sections, and any changes in mood that they suggest. Like standing at a distance in an art museum, get a feeling for the entirety of the work, leaving the details aside for now.

Begin the next stage: Learning the Piece

It is important, when beginning to actually learn to play a piece, to follow certain guidelines.

• Select the first phrase. Many new learners try to learn too much at a time. It is important that the first section be relatively short — say, four bars long.

• Note the key signature and the time signature and play the rhythm alone, always hearing the steady beat of the meter. Do this at a slow tempo, perhaps on one note at a time, as was suggested in the chapter "A Sound Beginning". Your goal is to play the rhythm steadily and accurately. If you learn the rhythm of a passage incorrectly, it is often very difficult to correct.

• One hand at a time, look over the rise and fall of the pitch. Note any large intervals and chords. Write their names in your music with a pencil, if you feel you may have difficulty recognizing them later. Always be aware of the key signature to be sure you are reading the notes accurately. Remember, you are doing this one hand at a time.

• Now is the time to figure out, and write in the music, the fingering you intend to use on this passage. Often there is fingering supplied by the editor. It may or may not fit your hand.

• Generally fingering is chosen to facilitate playing the passage, but there are other reasons for selecting certain fingers. These may include playing a strong sound with a strong finger or facilitating the playing of slurs, ornaments, or passagework.

• Trying out the fingering while playing hands together is important, as coordination may be made easier with alternate fingering. Also, check to see if the fingering you chose will work as well at the performance tempo. This is an important step in learning to play your piece, and should not be underestimated. Once the fingering is chosen, stick with it, unless you have a very well thought out reason to change it.

• Pay attention to all the details written in the music. These include:

> • dynamics, indications of degrees of loudness and softness,

- articulation, which are accents, various lengths of staccato, slurs, phrase shapes
- tempo changes, as in ritards or accelerandos
- pedal indications

- When learning to play hands together, it is wise to further limit the size of your learning section to one measure plus the first beat of the following measure. When mastered, repeat the process starting with the second measure. When this has become easy to play, combine the two measures.
- Continue this way through the entire learning section. The coordination required in playing hands together is challenging and one must repeat the small sections many times in order to master them. Again the goal is to play slowly and steadily.
- Since you now have a feeling for the emotional tone of the piece, it is important to play your tiny slow section with as much musicality as you can. This will enormously increase your pleasure in practicing. Project the melody, shape the phrase, listen to the bass notes, feel the harmonic colors, dance with the rhythm. These will be refined at a later date, but it is important to include them in the earliest stages of practicing.
- Memorize the learning section as you practice it. Take advantage of having analyzed the rhythm, intervals, chords and the motions used to play the section musically, and commit it to memory. You may not remember the entire passage several days later, but you will remember much of it. Later on in the piece, when the composer repeats certain rhythmic, melodic or harmonic motives, you will already know them.

• Learn your entire piece this way. It does not take as long as it seems. Besides, as you learn new sections, you will enjoy going back to play the parts you have already mastered, and feel the beauty of the music. This is what makes practicing enjoyable. The pleasure one gets from playing the earlier sections gives encouragement to carry on and learn the rest of the piece. This is not too different from when one loses five pounds, one is inspired to lose five more.

Return to the Big Picture

You can now play your whole piece slowly and steadily, with a reasonable interpretation of its musical meaning. There are several steps remaining.

• If you haven't already done so, memorize your piece now, even if you don't plan to perform it from memory. Do this while the piece is still slow. Specific steps are discussed in a future chapter. As described there, you will feel much more spontaneous in your performance if the notes are in your brain and not only in your fingers. Even when reading the score, your eyes will find guide notes and will not have to digest everything written on the page.

• Work on increasing the speed of your piece after it is memorized. You can either do this slowly, by notching up the tempo on the metronome, or you can work again in the small learning sections, bringing them up to speed quickly.

• Now is the time to tape record your piece and sit back to listen as a member of an audience. Your ear will find some places that are played convincingly, and others that need more work.

What to Listen for

• Focus your listening on one aspect of the performance at a time.

Melody:
• Did the melody sing and project above the accompaniment?
• Were the phrases shaped well, rising to the climax and relaxing at the end?
• Could you hear phrase relationships that develop the long line of the piece?
• Was the tone of the melody warm? Joyous? Mysterious? Despondent?
• Did you highlight anything unusual in the melody?
• Was passagework clean?
• Did you bring out inner voices where present?

Rhythm:
• Could you feel the meter of the piece without accenting every downbeat?
• Did your rhythm give a feeling of life to the piece?
• Did you observe rests properly?
• Did you hold long notes properly?
• Did you highlight any significant changes in rhythm patterns?
• Is the tempo appropriate?
• Do passages rush or slow down where they shouldn't?

Harmony:
• Did your dominant chords feel tension and the tonic chords relax?

- Did you highlight the chords that give color to your music?
- Did your bass notes give an adequate foundation for the harmony?
- Did you treat key changes or harmonic surprises effectively?

Texture:
- Did you consider the vertical balance of dynamics, and decide which notes should be prominent and which less so?
- Did you create a special sound for passages in the treble register, different from those in the lower registers or those with a wider range of notes?
- Was your pedaling appropriately clean, avoiding blurs?
- Did your pedaling obscure significant rests?
- Did ornaments blend in with the melodic line as embellishments?
- Did your chords avoid a harsh percussive touch?
- Did you have a picture or a story that brings your piece to life?
- Could you sense the color in your piece, which stems from your imagination?

Physically:
- Did you feel tension while performing the piece?
- Did anything hurt?
- Were you aware of moving to the music while you played?
- Did you "sing" with your inside voice along with the music?
- Did you feel confident that your preparation was

solid and that you were free to express your musical ideas without worrying about technical problems or correct notes?

There are so many things to listen for, think about and feel. When, and if, you are ready to perform this piece for someone else, plan a "dry run" with an imaginary listener first. Remember that listeners are only interested in the musical message coming forth through the sound. They do not know the notes, nor do they care about them. Your total focus should be on the big picture, on expressing the music, and you must trust that the work you have done, all those details, will all be there when you need them. Only at that point do practicing and performing become wonderful fulfilling experiences.

Success is a Journey, Not a Destination

As wonderful as it is to play an effective performance, the real joy is in exploring and discovering the tiny details that create the beauty of the music. This is done during preparation, which is the journey. Music comes alive only when a performer recreates it. The notes are only black dots on a page; the real music is in the sound. When a composer's inspiration and craft is combined with the emotions and life experience of a performer, music conveys a powerful message to the listener. Providing us with lifelong learning, the study of music is eternally invigorating and enriching.

Creativity in Early Piano Lessons

On the other side of the door
I can be a different me.
As smart and as brave and as funny or strong
As a person could want to be.
There's nothing too hard for me to do,
There's no place I can't explore
Because everything can happen
On the other side of the door.

On the other side of the door
I don't have to go alone.
If you come, too, we can sail tall ships
And fly where the wind has flown.
And wherever we go, it is almost sure
We'll find what we're looking for
Because everything can happen
On the other side of the door.

[written by Jeff Moss. "Teaching with Fire, Poetry that Sustains the Courage to Teach." Sam M. Intrator and Megan Scribner, editors]

Wouldn't it be wonderful if all students could feel this free as they step through the door into our studio? Wouldn't it be wonderful if they could climb into their imagination and sail tall ships, fly where the wind has flown, back, perhaps, a few centuries to when Bach was alive?

Creativity is all about tapping into one's imagination.

Consider two types of creativity: one in the interpretive realm, applied to music written by others, and the other in original student music, either improvised or composed. This chapter discusses both types of creativity in three different teaching arenas: the initial interview, the private lesson and the group class.

There is, however, a third type of creativity, and that is teacher creativity. Many teachers offer creative practicing incentives, compose unique exercises to solve technical problems, devise unusual recital themes etc. These are wonderful and are to be encouraged, but they cannot replace student creativity.

How can we enter a child's world and tap into his naturally creative way of looking at life? We are all aware of how much pleasure little children get from drawing pictures, making up stories and skits. They love to dress up and pretend they are someone else. Have you ever watched a child create an imaginary friend with whom she has lengthy conversations and can play with for hours? If we can only open the door, young students will be eager to color music with their vivid imagination.

Test creativity in the student interview.

When we meet a prospective student for the first time, we often size up musical abilities by testing rhythm, pitch, musical memory, knowledge of fundamentals, personality, but how often do we assess imagination?

By doing so in an interview, we essentially tell the new student that music study encompasses more than playing the right note at the right time – that using one's imagination in performing is not only fun but can transport us into the composer's world.

How can you assess imagination in an interview? Play something for the child and ask him to think of a title for the piece. Play a piece, or a part of a piece, that he might himself play someday, like "The Wild Horseman", by Robert Schumann, "Toccatina" or "Fairy Tale" by Dmitri Kabalevsky or "Distant Chimes" by Jon George. You need to reassure him that you don't expect him to actually know these pieces, but just to listen to them and think what they might be describing. If your only response is silence, which sometimes does happen, then give two or three choices of titles and let him select one. Then ask him a few other questions about what he heard.

Improvise in the student interview.

Another idea comes from the world of improvisation. Many teachers use an echo clapping game to assess whether the new student can remember rhythm patterns. As a variant of this activity, you might clap a simple four beat phrase and ask him to clap back an answering four beat phrase that is slightly different from the one you clapped. Teach him that he just clapped back a "variation" of your phrase and that composers use variations in music quite often. If a child does not know what to do, you may have to clap both the question and the answer phrase as a demonstration. Children will have fun doing this, and will recognize that having fun is part of music study.

Incorporate creativity into the private lesson.

How can we fit creativity into the private lesson when much attention must be given to correct notes, rhythm, fingering, dynamics etc.? In her booklet called "That's a Good Question", Marienne Uszler refrains from telling the student much of anything, but instead draws out information, observations and opinions from her student during the lesson. She advises asking linked questions, following one question with another one, which delves deeper and deeper into the music.

Open ended questions, as she describes so well in her book, begin with the words "Why?..., What if?..., Can you?..., Is it possible to?..., How else could you?..., Have you ever wondered?.... The answers that follow these questions reveal how the student is thinking, in fact, encourage the student to think. There can be several valid answers to these questions, and the discussion is apt to veer off in a direction the teacher did not anticipate. Creative responses increase student involvement and motivation.

Teach creative thinking.

This leads to the area of 'creative thinking' in music. Asking the student to alter the composition in some way encourages him to become more aware of what choices the composer actually made. For example, if you ask your student to end the piece with the dominant chord rather than the tonic and then describe what difference this would make, he becomes instantly more aware of tension and resolution inherent in certain harmonic progressions. If you ask him to transpose the piece into the minor, to move the trill from the cadence to another part of the piece, and then evaluate the results of what he did, he will have a more intimate understanding of why the composer wrote as he did. He may even come up with a better idea. The goal is to stimulate your student's curiosity, to involve him in thinking about the music he is playing.

Another technique many teachers may already use is to ask a student to create a story to go with the music. Sonatinas present a wonderful opportunity for this approach because of the contrasting sections of sonata allegro form. The use of imagery can make many pieces come alive.

Encourage creativity through improvising.

Improvisation can be taught easily in the piano lesson, and if the student is so inclined, this can lead to composing. Initially, one can improvise varying left hand accompaniment styles to a given melody in the right hand. These might include arpeggios, offbeat chords or jazz rhythms.

Improvise original music with the pentatonic tones of the black keys where all combinations of notes blend well together. Suggest titles to stimulate your student's musical imagination. Encourage him to use the pedal and explore all ranges on the piano to create different effects.

Consider using published compositions as a springboard. Jon George's "Day in the Jungle" is an excellent model for animal pieces. First, analyze how the composer wrote his piece. Noticing that he chose the chromatic scale to describe a beetle, a student might borrow this idea for his insect piece.

Improvising differs from composing.

When improvising, a student's piece can change every time it is played. When composing, he must remember the motives of the piece and be able to recreate them. Often structure becomes more important in a composition and it is an opportunity to learn about ABA form, motives and their variations, sequences etc. Students often need help in writing their pieces down. New computer programs such as Sibelius, Finale or Scorewriter help them do this.

When students create games they learn quickly.

In the areas of learning music fundamentals or facts about composers, students enjoy creating games themselves, in addition to those the teacher presents, which can be found in catalogs such as

Friendship House. Some student-made games might end up being long and tedious, but the learning that takes place while a game is being created, makes the activity worthwhile.

Opportunities for creativity in Piano Classes

A teacher should not overlook fostering creativity by working with groups of students. Classes can either supplement the private piano lesson or be the main vehicle of instruction. Children remember best when they participate in interactive group learning.

Creative activities in piano classes

• **Historical musical styles**: Ask students to listen to a Baroque piece ahead of time and come to class prepared to discuss it. Prepare some open-ended questions to advance the discussion. You might ask them to compare the form of this piece to a sonatina.

• **Accompanying:** Assign students a Christmas carol or other song to accompany the class in group singing. They should prepare their own accompaniment from a lead sheet. Show them how to do this.

• **Composers**: Ask each student to research a composer and come to class where other students will interview him.

• **Composition:** Have a student present a piece he has written. Class members then discuss how this piece compares with others they are studying.

• **Orchestration**: Ask each student to prepare a rhythm band accompaniment to a piece he is playing and write out the rhythm accompaniment so it can be performed in class.

Each of these ideas may encourage you to think of others.

Creativity belongs in music lessons.

There are so many ways to incorporate originality in student interviews, private lessons and group classes. Doing so will invigorate the curriculum for both student and teacher and make learning both more personal and more long lasting. It is also an excellent way to individualize music instruction by involving the student and his ideas directly.

We do our students a big favor by encouraging original thinking in their music lessons. These days more and more adults are seeking fulfillment in jobs that incorporate creativity. They value brainstorming, problem solving and opportunities for leadership over routine tasks. Experts say this will be even more true in the future as routine tasks are outsourced to lesser paid workers in other countries. I believe that adult creativity has its beginning in childhood. If we foster original thinking among our students, the implication for their future lives is enormous.

Developmental Barriers to Learning

It is often surprising to someone who plays the piano well how difficult it can be to teach this skill to others. Certainly children with talent and with musically supportive families can and do learn easily, but with other students, a teacher can run into roadblocks that were not at all expected.

Children with identifiable learning or emotional problems are a challenge to teach, as are students who have transferred from another studio where the basics were insufficiently mastered. But just as common are students with minor lags in maturity that can affect their ability to concentrate, to follow directions and to practice effectively. They must be guided individually in order to learn to their capacity.

Examples:

Michael has a short attention span.
He cannot concentrate for very long or focus his attention on a particular concept. This is common in young children but becomes a problem if the student is no longer young. Investigate, by talking with parents, to discover if there is a physical reason behind

this deficit and if the problem also evidences in school. Often a piano teacher, working one-on-one with students, can detect problems sooner than school teachers or even parents.

• A change in lesson time may be the answer. Students understandably get tired being in school all day, and they may have difficulty concentrating at a music lesson if it comes right after school, or if they are tired at the end of the day. It can be delicate to discuss these issues with parents, though they may appreciate your caring attitude.

• If concentration is a problem at the lesson, it is most certainly also a difficulty during the practice session where the child must direct his own work. Enlist parents to reduce distractions from siblings, television, telephone etc. Devise Practice Charts where the student can keep track of his own progress during the week, writing down or checking off what he has accomplished.

• Give guidance on how to make practice sessions goal oriented, using short-term goals that are easily mastered, and then recording them on the practice chart. Children who tape record their practice at the beginning and at the end of the week may be inspired by the progress they have made.

• Variety is very helpful with this student. Provide "off the bench" activities as well as those at the keyboard. Use mechanical, electronic and audio-visual equipment within the lesson, such as the metronome, a tape player, stopwatches, rhythm instruments and CD's. Let the student turn them on and off to keep his attention on the task at hand.

Alternate playing and listening to the beat of a

metronome. Measure speed in reading flashcards with a stopwatch. Using a tape recorder, have the student record and listen to one hand while playing the other.

• When a student uses rhythm instruments to accompany the teacher playing his piece, he will physically feel the rhythmic movement of the music. Enlist the student's help in making new flash cards, games and puzzles. Improvising question and answer phrases will keep the student's interest or regain it if he has drifted off. Occasionally sharing part of a lesson with another student can be another way of introducing variety to the lesson itself.

• If you know your student well, you can relate music to other parts of his life. Sports offer many parallel experiences: the desire to be as good as one can be; the need for drill and practice under the guidance of a coach; the pride of achievement.

• Keep directions simple, tackling one problem at a time. It can be confusing to the student to be told to play steadily, slowly, with a good hand position, proper fingering and dynamics. Music really is this complex, but a child with a concentration problem can't absorb it all at once. Praise attempts at improvement even if the results are not perfect. <u>Reward improvement, not just perfection.</u>

Luke is over-dependent on the teacher.

He leans on the teacher too much and must be "spoon-fed". This child needs a stronger self image if he is to develop enough confidence to trust his own judgments and learn from them. In monitoring his education, allow him to make an occasional wrong decision so that he can learn from his own misjudgments.

• In working with this student, encourage him to take part in his own instruction. For instance, he could write his own directions, make his own fingering decisions, determine his own practice techniques, warm-up routines and length of assignment. When progress occurs, point out that it is the result of his own decisions. Teaching like this may be more permissive than usual, but remember you are doing it to increase his involvement in learning music.

• Ask him to evaluate his own performances. Encourage him to discover the reason for errors. As he realizes that he is the master of his own progress, his self-confidence will grow.

• This student, in learning to affirm his own independence, may occasionally contradict his teacher. Though this may be hard to live with, we must realize that he cannot be independent and submissive at the same time. We need to understand that the negative responses may, in fact, be evidences of growth in his self-confidence.

This student may profit from helping other students, perhaps in a class or a shared lesson, or with a younger student in an ensemble.

Rob is an impatient child, one who is always in a hurry.

He wants to get the job done quickly, not necessarily accurately, carefully or thoroughly. He is apt not to take enough time to catch tricky rhythm patterns, check key signatures or observe clefs. He assumes that he immediately understands what to do without planning ahead. This child needs to gain appreciation for the relationship between details and the whole task.

• Such a student is often quite enthusiastic and it is helpful to build upon this. A teacher must help him examine the music before actually playing. He should describe what he sees in the score, before attempting to play.

• Plan the learning procedures he is to follow during home practice. Indicate how much time he is to spend on each piece or technical skill. Assign several activities that reinforce the same concept, such as grouping several activities in the same key (technical work, repertoire piece, transposing exercise, writing exercise). Use a tape recorder to evaluate practicing progress.

• Above all, model the behavior you wish to see in your students. You must show the same patience you expect your students to develop. Progress may be made in small steps. One cannot change impulsive behavior all at once. Each time this student acts with deliberation, he is a step closer to the goal of accurate learning.

Neena is lacking in motivation.

She needs to develop her own initiative for learning rather than expect others to stimulate motivation through rewards or prizes. Some students are passive receivers. One might say that the school system encourages this kind of learning. Students are trained to do as they are told. In music, if they show more individual initiative, their lessons might have more value.

• Sometimes these passive attitudes reflect the home atmosphere. Parents may not realize that their own non-involvement may be interpreted as negative toward classical music. Ask parents to become more supportive of their child's music instruction. They may be unaware of how their active interest can encourage their child's progress.

• Encourage students to perform at school or at church. Assist them to accompany the choir. Teach them popular music to play for their friends. Help them relate to the outside world as musicians and you will reap the benefits in the studio.

• Elicit their ideas and opinions. Withhold your opinion until you have heard theirs. This may lead them to take more ownership of their own musical education.

Helen suffers from a fear of failure.

She gets emotionally upset and anxious at any performance, and consequently is unable to do her best. This may also happen during tests at school.

Often a teacher wants to calm her fears by saying "We all get nervous". This may be true, yet many people ride over these fears and produce a good performance despite the nerves. It is better to offer a supportive smile, emphasize with her feelings, while teaching her how to relax through stretching and breathing deeply. Being nervous does not have to be a negative thing. Try to redirect the nervousness and transform it into usable energy.

• Let this student perform in a low-pressure environment, perhaps a piano class where the focus is on the style or structure of the music rather than on the performance. Present her at a younger class where students will be delighted to have an older visitor, or give a recital at a retirement home where residents are excited to hear children play.

In more relaxed environments, students will learn

to live with pressure. They will see that mistakes are inevitable but seldom fatal. Give encouragement but not unwarranted praise. Frequent opportunities provide many chances to improve and earn the teacher's praise.

• Select repertoire that sounds more difficult than it actually is, such as pieces built on patterns or with many repeating sections. Plan several practice performances before the "real thing" so that she becomes comfortable and confident.

Dylan blames others for his misfortunes.

He insists that the piece is too hard, or he has not had enough assistance, or he is overworked at school. He must learn that what happens to him is under his control.

• First check to see if his claims are valid. Perhaps the piece was too hard for him or for his available practice time. You must be sympathetic to this.

"Tell me where you need my help". This encourages the student to become aware of what he can and cannot do independently.

• Involve the student in planning the curriculum and have him commit to completing agreed upon tasks. Let him help select his repertoire and impress upon him that results depend mainly on his efforts.

Take on the Challenge.

There are several ways to maximize motivation for a child who has learning barriers in the study of music.

• First of all, take a personal interest in the student. Accept him where he is now and invite him to grow, both musically and personally. Give him your undivided attention during the time of the lesson, with no interruptions from small children or the telephone.

• Make progress during the lesson itself. Be sure he understands all concepts and that he knows what to do at home. Practice sessions should reinforce the learning that has already taken place at the lesson.

• Consider his feelings by including music he wants to play in his assignments. By satisfying his current desires you will be in a better position to build skills for more mature playing in the future.

• Always uphold high standards. Know that he will not always reach them, but don't let this on to the student. Praise him when he tries. Above all, have patience. It will take time to make progress but neither you nor the student will ever forget the experience of working together.

"Once Upon a Time..."
Presenting a Story Recital

Have you ever known anyone who didn't love a good story? And have you noticed how effectively the right music enhances the plot of a good movie? By weaving student recital pieces in and among the lines of a story, teachers can create recitals that engage the imaginations of everyone present.

• There are many reasons for presenting student recitals in the format of a story. First and foremost, it focuses attention by the performer as well as the listener on the expressive quality of the music, and away from the performer. Nervousness about missing notes practically disappears.

The music is chosen to enhance the action of the story line. At the point where the plot is exciting, the music chosen may have strong accents and dynamics. If the story describes a peaceful scene, the accompanying music may be gentle, atmospheric or lyrical. Student performers enjoy improving the expressive quality of their music as they learn and perfect their recital pieces.

• Children love Story Recitals. The students become a team, similar to the way a school play encourages cast members and stage crew to work well together. Friendships are made, as are wonderful memories of music lessons.

Parents and friends in the audience, rather than listening only for their own children, become fascinated by the entire program and may, as a result, develop a clearer understanding of the attraction and power of music. In fact, having had their imaginations stimulated, they may seek out adult concerts and listen for the "stories" suggested by symphonies, operas or chamber music.

• Having decided to try a Story Recital, you may first wonder how to begin. Start with a published story like "Peter and the Wolf", the "Nutcracker", or "Hansel and Gretel". Or you may ask the students to suggest a story.

Several publishers produce student versions of "Peter and the Wolf". Assign the parts of Peter, the Grandfather, the Wolf, the Bird, the Duck, the Cat, and the Hunters to students whose ability matches the level of the music. In the Schaum edition, Peter has many short snippets to play, whereas the Bird has only a few. In this case, give the role of Peter to a more advanced student, and the Bird to someone with less experience. Assign the other parts with similar criteria in mind. It is always possible for one student to play more than one part, or for you to take one of the more challenging roles.

Ask the students to memorize their parts. When they know their music by heart, they will play more expressively and perform more securely. Have the teacher, a parent or a non-performing student narrate the story.

My studio has presented "Peter and the Wolf" several times at local elementary schools. We perform for the kindergarten and lower grades, exhibiting how much fun music lessons can be. The children have made headdresses to show which character they are playing. They all wear similar T shirts in lieu of a costume.

• You can also make up your own story or put together your own assortment of music to illustrate a published story. An example of the latter that has been very popular in our studio, was adding our own selection of Spanish style music to the story of "Ferdinand the Bull" by Munro Leaf. Music by William Gillock, Lynn Freeman Olson, Glenda Austin, David Karp, Catherine Rollin and others describe the many moods of this timid bull as he is lured into the bull ring by ambitious matadors.

• In a different vein, we used patriotic songs from our country's rich musical heritage to accompany a story in verse about the founding of our nation. This story, "In 1776", written by Jean Marzollo, is typical of stories found in the children's section of a public library. Though our particular musical arrangements were written by me, many student publications of patriotic songs can be purchased at music stores.

You can also select music from the intermediate classical literature to enhance a story. Try illustrating "Where the Wild Things Are" by Maurice Sendak with accompanying music by Schumann, Kabalevsky, Burgmuller and Shostakovich.

Almost any story will work if it is not too long, has a variety of moods within it, and is appealing to young children.

• Depending on how quickly students learn, and how much other music they are studying at the time, allow from six weeks to four months for this project. Since you know the children's strengths, it is best for you to choose the story and read it to the children at the start of this adventure. Students meet several times in a workshop to try out what they have learned. This will inspire the others to learn and memorize their parts as well.

Involve the parents in several ways.

• Have them secure permission for their children to be released from their school, if the performance is on a school day.
• Ask them to help with whatever costume the child will wear. For a performance of Peter and the Wolf, we have found that jeans with white tee shirts and a simple headdress representing the character works well.
• Ask one of them to narrate the story.
• If desired, let one of them help children provide props or paint a mural as a setting for the story.
  The performance usually takes around thirty minutes and is best scheduled at the end of the school day when it will not conflict with academic subjects. Contact the school's principal and the music teacher early in the year to include this event on their calendar. At the beginning of the program, introduce the student performers to the audience, telling their age and the school they attend. Emphasize how much fun these students have had preparing this musical story, and encourage the young audience members to consider taking piano lessons.

• As an alternative, story recitals can be presented to the families and friends of the performers, or for residents at a local retirement home. An elderly audience thoroughly enjoys seeing the creative achievements of young students.

Teachers who have tried this type of recital often prefer it to the traditional format, because of the excitement it generates. Children are anxious to do it again. Because of this experience, they give added attention to the expressive elements in all their pieces, not just the ones in the story. Clearly this is what we desire.

He Didn't Practice Again!!!

"This is the third week in a row. How can I teach him anything if he doesn't ever practice? I used to like this kid, but I'm starting to dread his lessons. Every week I tell him again and again that you can't learn an instrument without practicing. And every week he comes in unprepared. This one student ruins my whole day!"

Sound familiar? Have you ever felt this way? Do you blame this on the student's lack of interest, the parent's lack of support, the society's lack of priorities? You might consider taking some of the blame yourself, for not considering how to deal with the problem.

Lecturing rarely works. Practicing with the student can lead to "spoonfeeding". Students may become lazy and think, "Why should I suffer over this problem when my teacher will solve it for me?"

An "alternative lesson" is a golden opportunity.

How many times have we said that the 30- or 45-minute lesson is never long enough to teach all that we wish to teach? Here is our golden opportunity to pick up some of these other skills that get put on the back burner when we are working solely with technique and repertoire.

Before teaching an "alternative lesson", talk through the previous week's assignment to be sure the student understood what he was supposed to do. Sometimes we assume a student understands what we mean, when he really doesn't and is too shy to admit it. Have him explain to you what it is he needs to do this week and how he plans to do it. Give him another chance. Don't do his work for him. I would not suggest teaching "alternative lessons" very frequently. They are useful during particularly stressful practice weeks, but should not take the place or regular instruction.

Consider these suggestions for "alternative lessons".

ELEMENTARY LEVEL

• <u>Note Drill.</u> All elementary students can use more drill in note reading. Take this opportunity to play note-reading games with your elementary student. Watch his skill improve. Students love to play games.

• <u>Transposition.</u> Use a simple familiar tune or make one up. Teach him to transpose it into some or all of the 12 keys. For more fun, make up a secondo part for yourself and accompany him in this tune, ending with the dominant seventh of the new key. Show him how to play this tune around the circle of fifths.

• <u>Improvisation.</u> Creating music on the black keys is always a good beginning. Choose one of the keys as the tonic key for the first and last note of his tune. Provide a rhythm pattern as a dance accompaniment.

You might even choose a rhythm pattern from one of the pieces he is learning. In this way the improvisation will support the concept he is studying in his repertoire.

• Harmonizing. Beginning students can learn to play an open fifth in the bass clef for the tonic harmony (C-G) and a second (F-G) for the dominant harmony. Teach them that the tonic will accompany triad tones and the dominant non-triad tones. Play some five-note tunes for them to harmonize. These too can be transposed.

INTERMEDIATE LEVEL

Students at an intermediate level can do all of the above, though additional activities might also interest them.

• Sight-reading. Take four index cards and write one measure of rhythmic notation on each, using the same meter. Use this to reinforce knowledge of different meters or new combinations of sixteenth and eighth notes. Have the student mix these cards up, line them up on the music rack, and play them on the fifth note of a scale while you accompany him with a tonic-dominant broken chord bass. Mix the cards in a different order and do it again.

Make a duet from a simple solo by having your student read one clef while you read the other. Alternatively, have your student play with both hands the first beat of each measure, while counting the remaining beats and preparing for the first beat of the next measure.

• Key Signatures. Page through an anthology and ask for the key of each piece.

- <u>Structure.</u> Play a piece and ask your student to identify the similar and contrasting sections.
- <u>Critical listening.</u> See if your student can catch the wrong note or wrong rhythm you slyly sneak into your performance of a piece, while he is watching the score. This role reversal may teach him to be more aware of his own errors.

Ask your student to mark the dynamics into an unmarked score, according to what he hears when you play the piece for him.

ADVANCED LEVEL

- <u>Style.</u> Play two minuets (or waltzes, polonaises etc) for a student and ask him to describe the similar features in each. Play a piece from two contrasting historical style periods and ask him to describe the stylistic differences in the composers' writings.
- <u>Interpretation.</u> Play a piano recording for a student and ask him to describe what the artist is doing to create his own interpretation. Direct his attention to rubato, phrasing, tempo, dynamics, balance, agogic accents, articulation or other noteworthy aspects of the performance.
- <u>Tone Color.</u> Play a recording of music from another media, such as an orchestra, and direct his attention to instrumental tone color, dialogue, textural contrasts etc. Discuss similarities in style between this music and music he knows on the keyboard.

Use these golden opportunities to rekindle the enthusiasm of your student. He will be more motivated, and you will feel renewed by having saved your student from stopping lessons. Keep in close touch with parents so that they know and support what you are doing.

Learn it by Heart

Teacher as performer

Teachers who also perform in concerts are often aware of new ways to help their students master their music. Sharing learning tips with an ensemble partner is one of the best ways to crystallize these thoughts.

"Why do you play without the score?" people ask after hearing one of our memorized two piano concerts. What they mean is "Why subject yourself to forgetting a passage when playing in front of a live audience?"

The answer is often another question. "Which is more important, a heartfelt performance or a less expressive but note-perfect one? It is a matter of priorities. Is your life less meaningful because you make minor errors like forgetting to turn on the dishwasher, bouncing a check or putting too much salt in the soup?" Just as we prioritize what is more or less important in life, we also make those choices in music.

Why memorize?

Speaking as a performer of both memorized two-piano music and non-memorized chamber music, I feel much more free in the former to express my interpretation. True, if I should forget something, and occasionally I do, I must get back on track at the precise beat that my partner is playing. Fortunately we have studied the work in such depth that this becomes easy to do.

In a chamber music performance my eyes are always on the score, watching, not only my own part, but those of my partners, so that if one of them inadvertently skips a beat, I can skip right with him. This intense focus in performance keeps me from submerging myself in the music. Whereas I aim to play artistically, I sense a lack of freedom and spontaneity. Certainly there are some chamber music passages that I do memorize, but for the reasons mentioned above, I must still watch the score in a performance.

Consider these two general suggestions.

One does not have to be a duo pianist to study in depth by memorizing. This method works just as well for soloists who traditionally perform without the music. Two things are important.

First: Memorize early in the learning process, before you have developed a finger memory. This strengthens your knowledge of exactly what is written in the score, as you must analyze everything that is on the page.

Second: Memorize backwards, starting with the

final section of your piece. This is so the end of the piece becomes very secure.

Traditionally, one is least sure of what was learned last. The most comfortable part of the piece is often the beginning. Practicing backwards is a way of becoming sure that you know the whole piece equally securely. When learning a two-piano piece, we do this together, so that our ears become very familiar with the other player's part.

Eyes, Ears, Fingers and Brain

There are four ways to memorize music, with your eyes, ears, fingers and brain. We use them all, at different times and to different degrees. For me, using my ears is where I begin. Teachers need to determine the best order for their students.

One Process of Memorizing – an example

After sight-reading through a piece or section, noting its repeating and contrasting parts, and penciling in fingering decisions, start memorizing the final phrase. Hands separately, play it with the proper musical inflections, noting its shape, intervals, harmony, rhythm, fingering and performance directions such as dynamics, staccato, accents etc. Very slowly, memorize the phrase hands alone. Often one needs to repeat this many times.

To help concentration, sing the melody, while naming the intervals of large jumps, make up words to the rhythm, and write in the harmony or anything else that will help you remember what to play. Notate any relationship between the beginning of one phrase and the end of the previous one. This writing step is crucial as a reminder, for the next practice day, of the thoughts that helped so much today. Penciled notations are also very helpful when reviving an old piece.

So start with your ears, listening to the melody, even the melody of the accompanying hand, and follow it with your brain, which tells you what to write, as a memory aid, in the score.

When putting the passage hands together, begin to use your eyes, first on the page, and then on the keyboard. Limit yourself initially to one measure and one note over the bar line. In other words, memorize the phrase in parts. Some people have a photographic memory and can recall the notes on the page. If you cannot do this, notice the black and white key patterns on the keyboard, and the relationship on the keyboard between similarities in the left and right hand patterns. Look for chromatic passages, broken chords, major and minor intervals, and mark them in the score.

All of this learning should be at a slow tempo. Since your goal is absolute security, do not hurry this process. When your brain blanks out and you cannot remember what comes next, do two things. First, peek at the score and remind yourself what to do next, and secondly, say the correction out loud and look for other relationships on the keyboard that will remind you how to play accurately. Do not play the correction by reading it, but look again at the keyboard and recall the notes from memory.

Once a piece is completely memorized, is it necessary to go back to the score? Absolutely. This is the time you will pick up details you may have missed during your initial learning process. Look carefully for phrases, accents, slurs, staccatos, rests, pedal markings, changes in tempo or dynamics. Since your brain and fingers know the notes, your eyes will be free to discover previously overlooked performance directions.

Eventually, that fourth dimension of memory, the fingers, takes over. Finger memory guides the successful performance. But if a mishap occurs, it is work you have done with your ears, eyes and brain that gives you the confidence to jump back into the music.

In reviewing music already learned, follow a similar process. First play the last page, refining any details that need work, then the last two pages and on back to the beginning of the piece. Since you are always moving into a section you have just played, your confidence will grow along with the piece. Practice many starting places within the piece and be sure to mark them in the score.

Can students learn this way?

Sure, if they are willing to try it. For some, who always wish to play from the beginning, it is counterintuitive. But for others who are willing to try a method that is new and different, the results are amazing.

A colleague has said that memory is not about remembering the notes, but knowing what to do when you forget them. Students who rely completely on finger memory, and many do, have no way to fix a memory slip. If they had analyzed their music as they learned it, they would recognize how to jump back successfully. Fingers, by themselves, have no brains.

Playing by heart has always meant performing

without the score. To me it means playing from the heart and I believe memorizing music allows you the freedom to do just that.

Why Study the Classics?

In the popular culture today, music is a strong communicator. It captivates our young people, listening on their Ipods, it dominates our TV's and radios. If popular music defines this generation, why do we persist in teaching our students Bach and Beethoven? What relevance does their music hold for our young people's development?

As technology affects our daily lives at an ever-increasing rate, it is important to remember that human nature remains constant from one generation to another.

In all centuries, and all over the world, people have fallen in love and have grieved over the death of friends and family. They have rejoiced when life went well and despaired when disappointments occurred.

The composers of our classical music speak to us as real human beings, with their joys and sorrows. When our students interpret their music today, they connect with the commonality of all mankind.

Consider Bach. He was a deeply religious man and dedicated his musical creations to the Lord. In doing so, he drew upon the best of his talent again and again. What a wonderful lesson he provides our students: to put your best effort into everything you do. One need not be religious to adopt this philosophy.

Consider Beethoven. He discovered at an early age a disability that could profoundly disrupt his chosen career as a musician. Though initially despondent over his progressive deafness, he rose above it and, despite the disability, became one of the strongest and most influential composers in our history. What a lesson he offers our students. Listening to and playing his music reminds us that we can excel, even when we suffer setbacks, if we summon up determination and persistence. The Fifth Symphony says it all; with it's impassioned first movement in c minor progressing to the glorious C Major Finale.

Bartok felt the need to preserve the melodies and rhythms of his native folk music. After transcribing much of this authentic music, he gave it new life by assimilating its unique elements into his serious compositions. Similarly our students dip into what is our national music, the blue notes and syncopations of jazz. They play Gershwin, Copland, Bernstein and others who have drawn upon elements of this American idiom.

One could go on. Those feeling nostalgic can find solace in the works of Chopin. Those who are shy can express themselves through music as Brahms did. Those who march to a different drummer can find models in Debussy.

Through studying the classics, just as they study literature, students will discover that human feelings are timeless even though the visible elements of civilization may change. It is a lesson worth learning and then passing on to future generations.

Introducing a Student to Brahms

When asked how he liked his new career as a piano teacher, my colleague mournfully said, "...but how do we get to Brahms? " Becoming painfully aware of the enormous distance between the elementary student literature and the masterworks we all hold dear, he wondered how to bridge this gap and arrive in the land of Brahms, Schubert and Chopin.

True, it takes several years before one can master Brahms' Intermezzi, Rhapsodies and Capriccios. These are advanced works and a student pianist must have much experience before tackling them.

An Introduction to Brahms

Brahms has given the advancing pianist a set of pieces that can lead the way to his more difficult works. These are the sixteen Waltzes of Op. 39. They feature many of the same challenges as his well-loved character pieces but in a much shorter form. Originally written for piano duet, they immediately became so popular that Brahms rewrote them as piano solos, and yet again, responding to popular demand, as simplified piano solos, without all the octaves. A pianist who learns to play the waltzes as solos, encounters many of the difficulties of his later works. He will soon be ready for the Intermezzi, Capriccios and Rhapsodies.

When teaching a student to interpret the classics, a teacher can take one of two approaches. Either analyze how the composer used melody, rhythm and harmony in his work, or appeal to the student's expressive imagination. This chapter on Brahms takes the analytic approach, whereas the following chapter on Chopin discusses the imagination's role.

Challenges in playing the music of Brahms

Brahms' musical style presents challenges in three areas: reading, technique and interpretation. In terms of reading, nine of the sixteen waltzes are in keys of four or more sharps or flats. Most have accidentals as well. This means a pianist must be able to read easily in all keys. The texture is chordal, requiring harmonic reading (vertical) as well as melodic (horizontal). Study the harmonies and harmonic relationships in order to interpret these with meaning.

Rhythmically Brahms plays tricks with duple and triple meter, sometimes alternating them, sometimes presenting them simultaneously. It helps to be an excellent reader, so that learning the notes is not too overwhelming, because it is only the starting point in an expressive Brahms performance.

Technical problems abound in these pieces, and your student may wish to practice specific exercises to speed up mastery. Octaves are everywhere, especially three and four note octave chords with other notes between the outer-voice octave. It is important to learn to play these without tension and to voice the melody note so that it sings above the rest. It is important to learn to anticipate the next chord shape in your hand.

Double notes and Inner voices

Double notes are common, especially double thirds and sixths. These too require careful voicing. Since Brahms' piano was the same full size as our modern instrument, his music covered much of the keyboard, creating leaps which can be treacherous if not learned securely. Similarly his dynamic range matched the expressive capability of his instrument so one must be able to produce a wide range of sounds from the very soft to the very loud and all levels between.

Being enamored of Bach's works, Brahms loved polyphony. Look for many passages with inner voices, bass line voices and contrapuntal melodic lines. Even the Waltzes, which were meant for a popular audience, give evidence of this complexity. The saving grace is that the Waltzes are short and therefore the technical difficulties are not too numerous.

The interpretive challenges are also substantial. It is necessary to analyze the music to truly understand the relationships that will bring the music to life. The following concepts of expressive playing are worth learning, as they apply to music by other composers as well.

Consider these ideas relating to rhythm:

• We know that the meter of a piece indicates the generally understood pattern of strong and weak beats. In a waltz we expect the first beat to be strong and the other beats to be considerably weaker. Sometimes the surface rhythm (the note value patterns) reinforces this, as in Waltz No. 15, where the longest note is always on beat one. Sometimes, though, it contradicts this, as in the middle section of Waltz No. 1 where all note values are the same. Listening to the even note values, it is hard to distinguish the downbeat, because the accompaniment pattern in the left hand contradicts the triple meter with its own duple rhythm. Study this ambiguity and decide which meter should be more prominent.

Brahms Waltz No. 1 m.9-12

• The downbeat is the strongest beat of a measure, but not all downbeats are equally strong. For example, in Waltz No. 3, the downbeat of measure 1 is stronger than the downbeat of measure 2. In this case the difference in pitch between the successive downbeats determines the interpretation.

Brahms Waltz No. 3 m. 1-4

Phrase shapes and relationships

• Good musicians think in phrases. They are aware of the shape of every phrase, making notes move toward the phrase's climax and relax after it. It is equally important to understand how phrases work together to build a larger structure.

• Explore phrase relationships, looking for questions and answers, repetitions and sequences. Examine repeated phrases to determine whether the repetition is an "echo", to be played softer, or a means of added emphasis, to be played louder. Look for variations and consider how they enhance a previous motive. Contrasting phrases require new sounds to call attention to new musical ideas.

• When two voices are in counterpoint, decide which is the predominant line. This is important in Waltz No. 16.

Harmonic understanding is always important in making interpretive decisions.

• Harmony to the composer is like color to the artist. The harmonies that blend together most naturally are the ones that are within the key of the piece.

• Harmonies meant to stand out, as accent colors, are those from a borrowed key, or those with added dissonances, as in Waltz No. 2.

Brahms Waltz No. 2 m. 9-12

• Color chords, like 7ths, augmented 6ths, are always significant and should be emphasized in performance, as in Waltz No. 2. This may mean playing them louder, or perhaps softer than the surrounding notes. Look also for unexpected chord progressions, as in Waltz No. 7. Consider whether the harmony patterns satisfy your expectation or offer a surprise. Convey this to your listener by your choice of dynamics or perhaps a subtle altering of the rhythmic flow.

Brahms Waltz No. 2 m. 13-16

A student who understands how the musical elements work in a Brahms waltz can apply those concepts to other music he studies. Working this way helps him become an independent learner.

The Brahms Waltzes provide an opportunity to study the composer's thought in depth. They give evidence to the 19th century love of the dance and were justifiably very popular when they were written. They also present a significant technical workout, and a test of one's reading skill. For all these reasons they are valuable study pieces. More importantly, they are grouped together into a wonderfully expressive set of pieces and deserve the popularity they have always had. Pianists are well rewarded when they explore this magnificent music.

Exploring the Chopin Preludes

The Chopin Preludes stimulate the musical imagination in both artist and student. These twenty-four short pieces, written in each of the twelve major and minor keys, catalogue a host of human emotions and exhibit a wide range of technical challenges. They can be performed individually, in small groups of several preludes, or as a complete set.

Suggestions for Practicing the Preludes

Slow practice is invaluable. Your fingers need to know securely every note in the piece because during a performance, your thoughts must be totally on the imagery, or what the piece is expressing. Practicing the faster preludes in altered rhythms is helpful for building relaxation. For unraveling inevitable snags, try a change of fingering. Mentally regrouping a passage, or altering the way you think of the clauses within a phrase, can ease a problem. Though pedal is important in performing this music, legato is improved by practicing without pedal.

Barbara Wing

History of the Preludes

Chopin wrote these pieces in the decade of the 1830's and they reflected much of what was going on in his life. He was born in 1810 in Poland and educated in Warsaw. When he decided to pursue a musical career, he travelled to the musical capitals of Europe, much in the way that young artists flock to New York City today.

He first went to Vienna, where he had made a successful impression a few years before, but this time was not welcomed there. So he moved on to Paris in 1831, feeling despondent after being rejected, homesick because he did not know anyone in Paris, and worried about troubles at home.

Poland was under the autocratic rule of the Russian czar. An underground group of freedom fighters, which included some of Chopin's friends, tried to reclaim their homeland by staging an uprising against the Russians. This was beaten down right at the time of Chopin's arrival in Paris. He expressed his despondency by sketching out his first two Preludes, No. 2, a very despairing piece and No. 24 a defiant one, in the mood of the Revolutionary Etude.

The rest of the Preludes were written during the next seven years. His life in Paris had its ups and downs. Chopin was welcomed into high society and taught many of the ladies and their daughters, some quite talented. His music was highly regarded and the few concerts he gave in lovely salons were packed. But his health was never good. He suffered from tuberculosis, which he had contracted as a child and death was never far from his mind.

In 1838 he traveled to Majorca with his new friend Georges Sand, to spend the winter in a warmer climate, with the hope that his health would improve. Unfortunately it was a cold rainy winter and his health worsened. He did, however, have his beloved Pleyel piano shipped to him, and was able to complete the Preludes. They were published in 1839 with a dedication to Pleyel, his good friend and manufacturer of his piano. Both Schumann and Liszt extolled his genius as revealed in these wonderful miniatures.

Chopin's relationship to the music of Bach

Why would someone want to write a set of pieces in each of the major and minor keys? In Chopin's case, it might have been an homage to Bach, who, one hundred years earlier, had written the "Well Tempered Clavier", a set of preludes and fugues in each of the major and minor keys. We know that Bach figured strongly in Chopin's education, that the only piece he brought with him to Majorca was the "Well Tempered Clavier", and that he had between 15 and 20 of Bach's preludes committed to memory. That's a fascinating fact since he performed only his own music in his concerts. He brought the Bach for study purposes.

One can also question why Bach himself wrote a set of pieces in each of the major and minor keys. Conventional wisdom tells us that Bach was exploring a new tuning system which allowed music to be written in keys with many sharps and flats as well as those with just a few. But Bach could just as easily have written one prelude and fugue and transposed it into many keys, which would demonstrate this tuning system just as easily. And why did Bach, twenty years later, write another set of twenty-four preludes and fugues, having already demonstrated this theory with the first set?

Perhaps there was another reason. Different keys, or tonalities, inspire compositions with very different moods or "affects". A piece written in D major has a very different emotional tone from one in F major, or C major. Perhaps both Bach and Chopin were fascinated with this, and wanted to explore this phenomenon through their own composition.

We know that Chopin was a very private person with no close confidants. He confided in his piano, and must have enjoyed expressing all his moods, from joy to despair, through sound. In his introduction to the Piano Method he was writing at the close of his life, he defined music as "thoughts and perceptions in sound". The preludes were his emotional diary, and we come to know Chopin as a person by playing and listening to the preludes.

These pieces are all very short, lasting on average two minutes or less. That is a very brief time to make a musical statement and is one of the challenges for the performer. They follow the circle of keys, beginning with the major and relative minor with no sharps, followed by 1,2,3,4,5,6 sharps and back through the flats. He did not compose them in this order, and we do not know if he performed all of them in this order, though most professional pianists these days do.

They have become favorites of so many pianists because of the opportunity Chopin gives for individual interpretation. Often there are no dynamic markings, only approximate tempo markings and ambiguities with melody and rhythm in the score, allowing the performer to decide what features are prominent, and which subordinate. Consequently, on listening to several artists' recordings of the Preludes, one hears significant differences of interpretation.

A Personal View on Selected Preludes

Prelude No. 1 in C major shows the direct influence of Bach in its structure. In his opening prelude to the "Well Tempered Clavier" Bach presents a short pattern as a building block, never deviating from this but coloring it with new harmonies which develop the architecture of the piece. Chopin follows this same procedure with his own building block, similar but slightly different from Bach's.

The piece is marked agitato, very different from the peaceful mood of Bach's work. The agitato is created by a conflict between the bass line, on the first beat of each bar, and the two presentations of the melody, one in an alto register, played by the right hand thumb, and the other an octave higher. It is unclear in the music which line should be most prominent so it is up to the performer to make this decision. It is also important to remember that this is the opening work of the set and it needs to have an introductory quality.

Prelude No. 4 in e minor paints a portrait of a depression. The tone is somber and the steady progression of minutely changing harmonic chords suggests the slow passage of time. The melody vacillates back and forth between two notes, a half step apart, suggesting a person completely devoid of energy. After an outburst at the climax, the piece ends as it began. Tone, phrasing, voicing and a vivid sense of imagery are all important in presenting an effective interpretation.

Prelude No. 6 in b minor resembles a cello solo because of the low register of the melodic line. It is a contemplative piece with beautiful harmonies climaxing with the unexpected and dramatic Neapolitan chord of C major. Singing tone, voicing and phrasing are its chief requirements.

Prelude No. 7 in A major is the shortest in the set and the simplest in terms of the notes themselves. To play them effectively requires good balance, pedaling and a singing tone. Like a gentle mazurka, the phrase moves toward the second measure. Its simplicity implies childhood innocence.

Prelude No. 8 in f# minor is a tempestuous, passionate etude. A pianist must initially figure out the relationship between the large and small notation. Unlike the Etude Op. 25 No. 1 in Ab major, where the small notes arpeggiate the harmony, in this prelude the small notes offer a contrasting rhythm to the left hand accompaniment, as well as many non-harmonic tones. This makes the small notes more important than in the former piece, contributing considerably to the piece's intensity. Nevertheless, the melody, played by the right hand thumb, should always be dominant. There is a wide dynamic range within the piece which is very effective when observed.

Prelude No. 9 in E major has a majestic character, created by the slow tempo, the rich low register and the full-textured solemn chords. Scholars disagree as to whether the melodic dotted eighth and sixteenth rhythm should be played simultaneously with the triplet of the harmony as in Baroque practice. Most pianists choose to play it the way it is written. Chopin's use of harmony is unique. Within this one page piece, he progresses from E major in the tonic opening to Ab major at the climax without it seeming unusual.

Prelude No. 13 in F# major suggests relaxing in a sailboat on a Sunday afternoon. The left hand ostinato recreates the gentle waves on the water, and the static right hand suggests that the boat is hardly moving. On the second page, a contrasting section in d# minor brings forth a wistful tune which melds with the main tune as the piece ends. Singing tone, voicing and careful pedaling are required.

Prelude No. 14 in e-flat minor describes a storm on the bay. Starting quietly, it builds with successive surges to a powerful fortissimo and then dies away. The entire piece is played in unison. Required are a large dynamic range and flutter pedaling.

Prelude No. 15 in D-flat major is the familiar "Raindrop Prelude". Imagine a narrative within this ternary form piece. The A section presents Chopin feeling quite comfortable in his Valdemosa monastery home on Majorca (where he wrote the piece) while his housemate Georges Sand and her children go shopping. A light rain begins, represented by the repeated A-flats in the accompaniment. In the B section, the A-flats turn to G#s as the skies become dark and the rain increases. There are thunder claps and lightning which frighten Chopin, alone in the monastery. He fears for the safety of the others. At long last the storm subsides and the others return. A small cadenza greets them and the piece ends quietly. Thinking through this, or a similar story, helps the performance come alive.

Prelude No. 20 in c minor is one of the most accessible ones in the set, yet requires a large hand and much tonal control. Its quarter note motion creates the air of a parade that is receding into the distance. A warm weight-produced tone, with focus on the outside notes, is best for the beginning. In line two, with a decrease in dynamic level, voice the top of the right hand chord, lightening the texture and apply the una corde pedal toward the end of the line. In line three, a repeat of line two, voice the middle of the chord, while still hearing the top melody. The crescendo at the end of this line need not return to a full forte, but should grow, with the final chord being quiet.

Prelude No. 21 in B flat major, marked *cantabile*, is a lyrical song floating above a double note, chromatic accompaniment. The difficulty lies in voicing and pedaling the accompaniment so as not to intrude upon the melody. Aside from this, the piece is quite accessible. It has a peaceful quality, similar to Prelude No. 13.

Prelude No. 22 in g minor is another dramatic shift in emotion. An octave etude, it presents a narrative which pits the left hand octave melody in a contest with the right hand interjections, all at a heightened dynamic level. Challenges include the many leaps, building a long melodic line, rubato and telling a dramatic musical story.

Prelude No. 23 in F major is a graceful portrait with a harp-like texture. The flowing right hand features a perpetual motion passage which creates the atmosphere. Below it the left hand sings a melody, punctuated by occasional trills. A fascinating feature of this piece occurs at the end when the peaceful F major arpeggio is disturbed by an unexpected E flat, turning the harmony into a questioning dominant seventh. Difficulties include creating the proper atmosphere by tonal balance, negotiating the left hand trills into the melody, and careful plucking of the above-mentioned E flat.

Prelude No. 24, in d minor, was quite possibly sketched out in 1831 when Chopin arrived in Paris and heard about the failure of the Warsaw uprising. It has a defiant nature which recalls the Revolutionary Etude. The right hand opening figure, a descending minor broken triad, is reminiscent of the opening of Beethoven's Appassionata sonata, which Chopin would have known. This becomes a significant motive in the piece, beautifully reharmonized in the major in the central part of the work. The right hand also presents some challenging and dramatic full-keyboard scales. All of this lies over the widely spaced left hand broken chords, which form the real difficulty of the piece. Avoiding tension in this dramatic piece is a real challenge. Quite unusually, the piece ends with three single note bass D's, which could possibly resemble gunshots. One can only imagine what might have been in Chopin's mind when he wrote this.

The Preludes are very effective when played as a set because of the contrast between the individual works. They are also effective when played in smaller groups, which is how Chopin might have performed them. As study pieces, they serve as mini-etudes, being shorter than the Op. 10 and Op. 25 etudes. But most importantly, they are some of Chopin's best works that are justifiably among the favorites of both amateur and professional pianists.

Postlude
Keeping the Love Alive

It is estimated that nine out of ten piano students quit lessons by the end of their second year. This is an appalling statistic, because these students could not have learned anything securely enough to be useful and lasting, and because they quit out of failure, frustration or boredom – hardly feelings we would want nine out of ten people to feel about music.

Every time a student leaves, one wonders if there was anything his teacher could have done to avert this happening. Sometimes there isn't anything the teacher could have done. It was the parent who registered the child for lessons, and perhaps the student's passion lies elsewhere. But before giving in to this, it is worth the teacher's time to examine her instructional program and think about different approaches.

A teacher has a unique opportunity to control the learning environment. Individually designed lessons can make almost every student successful. Starting off the fall season with an easily learned piece will capture the student's initial enthusiasm and prepare him for the more challenging pieces ahead.

Children often begin lessons because of their parents' wishes. This is not to be regarded badly. We need parental support if music education is to be successful. But very soon the teacher must switch the motivation from the parent to the child. The sooner the switch is made, the better.

Skills, Knowledge and Desire

Consider three dimensions in learning music: Skills, Knowledge and Desire. Teachers feel it is their proper role to teach the skills of reading and performing. They guide students in acquiring knowledge through music theory and literature. However, too often they feel students must come to them already brimming with a desire to learn. Desire, they feel, the third dimension, is not a responsibility of a teacher. I suggest that not only is it a proper role, but it is more crucial than the others, for without desire or motivation, a student will never acquire skills or knowledge.

Core requirements for excellent teaching

Teachers must select high quality music for their students to study. Fortunately there is a wide repertoire to choose from, and beautiful music need not necessarily be difficult. Choosing the right piece at the right time is a highly effective way to motivate a student. If a teacher fails to do this, his student may understandably stop lessons.

It is also important that your student perform his music to the best of his ability. His melodies need to sing, his rhythms need to dance and through his imagination he needs to create a musical image. When a student becomes involved with his music, it is doubtful he will lose interest in lessons.

It is very important to teach skills as well as repertoire. Some teachers work their way through study literature, without making sure that students have securely understood the skills involved. When the music becomes complex, a student may quit in frustration over not being able to understand the music accurately enough to learn it.

Suggestions to maximize student motivation

Try these ideas during private or group lessons. They are suggestions that will increase a desire to study music in depth.

Begin and end each lesson with joy

We often hear a parent say, "I want my child to enjoy music". Everybody wants to enjoy music, but how much joy is there in the average piano lesson or, the average practice session?

Start every lesson with something joyful so that an attitude of a shared musical experience sets the tone of the lesson. End with something joyful so that your student leaves with a feeling of exhilaration.

"What is the best thing you can do today?" "What would you like to play first?" It's the student's choice and it starts the lesson on a "high". It is fun to accompany a warm-up scale in duet fashion. Besides helping your student keep the beat, you will share an enjoyable moment. If your student does not know or care what he plays first, you might ask him where he needs your help. Tell him that when you go to a doctor, you don't make him guess whether you have a headache or a stomachache. That often gets a laugh. Show your student that you are his guide, and that you will find ways to help him be successful in piano playing.

A colleague of mine compared playing a piece with flying an airplane. As the takeoff and landing of an airplane are the most treacherous parts of the trip, she believed the beginning and ends of pieces are the most treacherous parts of the performance. Stretching the analogy, I believe that the beginning and ends of lessons are crucial to a positive student attitude and to maintaining a desire to study music.

There can be a wide gap between what a student can do now and what he wants to do, or between what he can do now and what he is expected to do by his next lesson. He may worry whether he has what it takes to be successful.

A Personal Anecdote

Several years ago I took a beginning German language class. I intended to complete all the homework faithfully, but I didn't always do it. I would come to my classes wobbly on the vocabulary, unsure of the grammar and scared that my teacher would ask me a question I couldn't answer in German. So what did I do? I quit. It is true I was very busy, but I doubt that was the real reason for quitting. I had no confidence in my ability to learn this language and my insecurity was reinforced each week. Immediately I saw the parallel between the language class and the music lesson.

Build students' confidence at every lesson.

How do we do that? When practicing a problem spot during a lesson, point out the growth that is occurring. "Ten minutes ago you couldn't do that!" Show them that they can learn and improve. Point out growth over the long haul also, because often they just don't see it.

Let one student teach another. The teaching student does not have to be super advanced, just more advanced than the other student. Helping another student solve a musical problem is an effective confidence builder.

Be instructional, not correctional.

When teaching in a correctional manner, you are being reactive. Your student plays and you react. "That was the wrong rhythm. You forgot the key signature. You ignored all the dynamics on the page". Learning in an atmosphere where every lesson is a test is no fun for either teacher or student.

A better way is to work musically with your student. "What is different about these two phrases? Is it the rhythm? How does that difference make you feel? How can we make the listener aware of this difference? Now you can see why the composer has indicated different dynamics for these two phrases".

Every lesson should emphasize the magic that is in music. Very often, with primary attention on the musical details, a student will correct his own mistakes. Praise him for this, and point out that his improvement was due to more focused attention, slower tempo, and smaller learning chunks. In this kind of teaching you are modeling better work habits – the kind you want him to use at home.

If there are too many corrections to be made, that is a signal to you that your student's reading skills are weak and need attention. Develop these skills outside of repertoire, in much easier music.

If you were the student, wouldn't you want the teacher to attend to your personal needs, questions and situation? This is how our students feel. They come to lessons with expectations of their own. We need to balance our curriculum needs with theirs. Choosing the right repertoire at the right time is one of the most important things we do. Whereas we need to be flexible in the kind and amount of literature we assign, we must remember never to lower our standards, or we will lose their respect.

Search out quality music and imaginative literature, especially in the early stages. Too many students quit because they are bored with the music they are assigned to practice. Ask a student which of several pieces he would like to play.

Treat elementary learners and intermediate learners differently.

Pay attention to the learning maturity of your students. Treat elementary and intermediate learners differently. An elementary learner must play his whole assignment at the lesson, so he leaves with the confidence of being able to do it. His task is to become more comfortable with these pieces and exercises at home.

An intermediate learner can be taught the concepts on one page or section, and be given responsibility to apply the concepts to a new page or section. An elementary learner needs to build up skills and confidence so he can become an intermediate learner. Transfer students, who may already be playing intermediate literature, might still be elementary learners. Work to build up their skills before expecting them to successfully take responsibility for independent learning.

Elementary learners need specific directions for practicing. Intermediate learners need options and can be given responsibility for choosing how to achieve certain tasks.

Use the power of group learning.

The supplementary group lesson is a powerful tool for maintaining a desire to study music. When friendships are made through music, motivation can increase dramatically. Students are inspired by their peers. "If he can do it, I can do it" is their maxim. They exude a cooperative spirit and are eager to help their classmates solve their musical problems. Ensemble develops teamwork, and many class activities develop leadership.

Vary your class activities so that all students shine at something. Let the group admire a talented performer. Let an intellectual student shine at analysis and praise another child for excellence in ear training. Always encourage the creative child and value his originality. Everyone benefits with the realization that there are many ways to excel in music.

Balance concentration with recreation.

If the private lesson is the work session, then the class can be for play. Use games, contests, teams, challenges, special events and guests. This is a time to share social music and encourage children to contribute their ideas to class plans.

Children learn in many different ways. A class offers opportunities to reinforce concepts with alternative teaching methods. Hands-on activities are especially effective in group settings. For example, when students conduct a piece of music, or march while they sing, they will learn more easily to feel a steady pulse.

Think about product and process-oriented instruction.

To understand process, think about a kindergarten. When children play, they are unaware of all they are learning. Their play is child-directed, without defined purpose, and creative, yet they are constantly learning about the world around them. The products they produce, the drawings and stories, are not as important as the process of making them.

When older children play, as in sports, their play is characterized by high energy and endurance, increased focus and concentration. Whereas a product is involved, as in winning a tennis match, it rarely diminishes the joy of playing itself.

How does this apply to music? In early childhood music classes, children learn through playing. They play by singing songs, dramatizing them, adding rhythms and movements. The teacher is a facilitator, whose role is to stimulate their imagination.

When the child advances to private lessons, there is a sudden shift in the learning environment. No longer child-directed, these lessons are teacher-directed. No longer without defined purpose, these lessons have a very specific purpose, which is to master correct reading and effective performance. No longer creative and different every time, these lessons stress repetition of a single concept until it is mastered. Students have lost a personal involvement in music making. Is it surprising that they quit?

What is the matter? Where is the problem?

• Do we start students in private instruction too young, forcing them to work when they need to play?

• Are the recitals and competitions, which all stress a performing product, too important so that we eliminate all time for exploratory music making?

• Do we stress skills and knowledge at the expense of desire?

• Is it possible to include process-oriented instruction in a traditional curriculum?

Sure it is. The teacher who encourages her students to sight-read, improvise, play by ear, harmonize is already doing this. The teacher who strengthens her students' knowledge of theory through games is also doing this. All of these activities can be done in a private lesson, but they are more fun in a class, where it takes on the aura of play. The spontaneous music making is fueled by the enthusiasm of peers. Studies show that these skills, not the recital skills, are what enable amateurs to carry music into their adulthood.

A teacher who leads class discussions about repertoire, encouraging students to conceptualize, analyze, react and evaluate is also using process-oriented instruction. In these activities, students can become just as absorbed in music as when performing.

We need to balance product with process-oriented instruction if we want to maintain a desire to study music.

• Look for ways to maximize motivation through both private and group lessons. When we enjoy students' achievements, we create a bond between teacher and student based on a shared love of music. This bond is not easily broken. It can last a lifetime.

• When we encourage their confidence, we develop trust: our trust in their innate musicality and capacity to learn; their trust in us as mentor and role model.

• When we empower them to become a partner in learning, and give them active control of their music making, they are far less likely to drop out of lessons. Sure, they may be busy, but they will make room for music.

If our goal is for students to enjoy music, they need to feel that pleasure right now. Provide an education that is fun, stimulating, challenging and rewarding. If students enjoy music now, they are likely to enjoy it for the rest of their lives. By assuming active responsibility for that third dimension, Desire, we can be sure this happens.

Recommended Reading

Active Learning – 101 Strategies to Teach Any Subject
Mel Silberman
Allyn and Bacon, 1976
Activities to use in music classes that stimulate student involvement and creative thinking.

Alternative Teaching Strategies: Helping Behaviorally Troubled Children Achieve.
Marshall s. Swift, George Spivak
Research Press, Champaign, IL 61820, 1995
Written for the classroom teacher, this insightful book offers ideas to individualize instruction.

More than Teaching: a Manual of Piano Pedagogy
Earle Moss
Gordon V. Thompson Music, Toronto, Canada, 1989
Combining lectures given at the University of Toronto and a lifetime of teaching and performing experience, the author offers advice on aspects of piano technique, solving common rhythmic difficulties, effective performance, lesson planning and cultivating musicianship skills.

Behavioral Profile of the Piano Student, including a New Look at the Cause and Prevention of Premature Drop-outs

Sidney Lawrence

Workshop Music Teaching publications, Hewlett, NY, 1978

Based on research projects conducted at his music school, the author describes the natural developmental and attitudinal ups and downs of the average young piano student and how the teacher should respond.

Making Music for the Joy of It: Enhancing Creativity Skills and Musical Confidence

Stephanie Judy

G.P. Putnam's Sons NY, 1990

A practical book for adult students that emphasizes the joy that can result from meeting a challenge. Includes a large section on practicing.

Sound Pictures, Books One and Two

Barbara Wing

P.O. Box 366, Cabin John, Md. 20818-0366

Two collections of expressive elementary level piano music that can be taught by ear or by reading to the beginning piano student.

Rhythm and Reading, Books One and Two

Barbara Wing

P.O. Box 366, Cabin John, Md. 20818-0366

A novel method of teaching music reading at the piano by isolating the reading of rhythmic phrases from the reading of pitch phrases. When students master these skills separately, before combining them, they make faster progress. Book Two contains five finger dances to harmonize and transpose, beginning hands together reading exercises and studies which illustrate the differences in historical styles.

Learning to Improvise
Barbara Wing
P.O. Box 366, Cabin John, Md. 20818-0366
A collection of activities which teach keyboard harmony and transposition as well as beginning improvisation.

Guide to Effective Practicing
Nancy O'Neill Breth
Hal Leonard Corporation
A comprehensive collection of practice techniques that will help students solve problems in accuracy, articulation, balance, continuity, coordination, evenness, expression, fingering, memory, pedal, rhythm and speed.

A Pianist's Approach to Sightreading and Memorizing
Beryl Rubinstein. Carl Fischer. 1950.
A manual with practical advice on improving one's skills of sight-reading and memorizing. The author emphasizes physical command of the instrument in all keys and a knowledge of musical elements that allows the pianist to speculate as to what is about to happen next in the music.

Questions and Answers: Practical Advice for Piano Teachers
Frances Clark the Instrumentalist Company, 200 Northfield Rd. Northfield, IL. 1992
Written by one of the most creative and influential piano pedagogues in the USA, this book addresses common

problems of teaching in a question and answer format. Her practical responses give evidence to her many years of experience and her advice is inspirational to both new and experienced teachers.

That's a Good Question 2003
Time Flies 2004
Play it Again, Sam 2003
    Marienne Uszler
    The FJH Music Company, Inc.

Three booklets that offer sound, practical advice on their particular topic. The teaching strategies recommended are immediately usable in the studio and will give a fresh vitality to all teachers, whether new or experienced.

A Piano Teacher's Legacy: Selected writings by Richard Chronister
    ed. Edward Darling
    The Frances Clark Center for Keyboard Pedagogy, Inc. 2005

Compiled from writings and lectures given during his all too short lifetime, these essays offer insights into what makes piano teaching truly effective.